Kandinsky, 1913

spannendsten Kapitel der modernen Kunst: Schrittweise werden die figurativen Elemente aufgelöst und Form und Farbe ›befreit‹. Aus der Erkenntnis, daß der »Bildgegenstand meinen Bildern schadet«, fand Kandinsky zu einer nie gekannten schöpferischen Freiheit. 1911 war er Gründungsmitglied des ›Blauen Reiters‹: die lyrischste unter den Spielarten des deutschen Expressionismus.

Seit 1917 mit einer russi-

freedom. In 1911, he cofounded the Blue Rider group, by far the most lyrical of the various schools of German Expressionism.

Having left Germany when war broke out in 1914, Kandinsky soon broke off his engagement to Gabriele Münter and married Nina Andreevskaya, the daughter of a Russian officer. From 1918 to 1921, he played an active part in the major debate on the politics of art which followed the social

---

18 Postkarten zum Heraustrennen
18 detachable postcards

---

schen Offizierstochter, Nina Andreevskaya, verheiratet, nahm Kandinsky 1918-21 in den nach der Oktoberrevolution neugeschaffenen Avantgarde-Institutionen der UdSSR leitende Funktionen wahr, danach wurde er Lehrer am Bauhaus in Weimar und Dessau. Sein Stil in dieser Zeit ist gegenüber der poetischen Intensität der Murnauer Jahre zu einer geometrischen Abstraktion versachlicht.

Kandinskys ambitionierteste Werke sind in Öl gemalt; parallel zu ihnen schuf er aber auch eine Vielzahl an Aquarellen und Zeichnungen, denen er große Bedeutung beimaß. Sind seine frühen Arbeiten auf Papier eher als Vorstufen zu später realisierten Bildern zu verstehen, so eröffnen sie von 1923 an als unabhängige Kunstwerke eine Periode der Innovation und des Experiments.

1933 übersiedelte Kandinsky nach Paris, wo er bis zu seinem Lebensende 1944 lebte und arbeitete.

and cultural upheaval of the Russian Revolution, but went back to Germany in 1922 to teach at the Bauhaus in Weimar and Dessau. Moving towards geometric abstraction, he steadily neutralized the poetic intensity of his Murnau paintings.

Kandinsky's most ambitious pictures are painted in oils, but he also produced a large number of watercolours and drawings. While most of his early works on paper are merely preliminary studies for paintings, this aspect of his art later took on a major importance in its own right as a medium of innovation and experimentation.

In 1933 Kandinsky moved to Paris, where he continued to reside and work until his death.

Wassily Kandinsky
Berg/Mountain, 1911-12
Privatsammlung/Private collection, © VG Bild-Kunst, Bonn, 1993

Aus dem Prestel-Buch/From the Prestel book:
Kandinsky, Aquarelle und Zeichnungen/Kandinsky, Watercolors and Drawings
(German and English editions) Prestel, München · New York

Wassily Kandinsky
Ohne Titel/Untitled, 1912-13
Privatsammlung/Private collection, Bern, © VG Bild-Kunst, Bonn, 1993

Aus dem Prestel-Buch/From the Prestel book:
Kandinsky, Aquarelle und Zeichnungen/Kandinsky, Watercolors and Drawings
(German and English editions) Prestel, München · New York

Wassily Kandinsky
Aquarell mit rotem Fleck/Watercolour with Red Spot, 1913
Deutsche Bank AG, © VG Bild-Kunst, Bonn, 1993

Aus dem Prestel-Buch/From the Prestel book:
Kandinsky, Aquarelle und Zeichnungen/Kandinsky, Watercolors and Drawings
(German and English editions) Prestel, München · New York

Wassily Kandinsky
Ohne Titel/Untitled, 1913
© VG Bild-Kunst, Bonn, 1993

Aus dem Prestel-Buch/From the Prestel book:
Kandinsky, Aquarelle und Zeichnungen/Kandinsky, Watercolors and Drawings
(German and English editions) Prestel, München · New York

Wassily Kandinsky
Aquarell für Poul Bjerre/Watercolour for Poul Bjerre, 1916
Privatsammlung/Private collection, Schweden/Sweden, © VG Bild-Kunst, Bonn, 1993

Aus dem Prestel-Buch/From the Prestel book:
Kandinsky, Aquarelle und Zeichnungen/Kandinsky, Watercolors and Drawings
(German and English editions) Prestel, München · New York

Wassily Kandinsky
Ohne Titel/Untitled, 1921
Öffentliche Kunstsammlung, Basel, © VG Bild-Kunst, Bonn, 1993

Aus dem Prestel-Buch/From the Prestel book:
Kandinsky, Aquarelle und Zeichnungen/Kandinsky, Watercolors and Drawings
(German and English editions) Prestel, München · New York

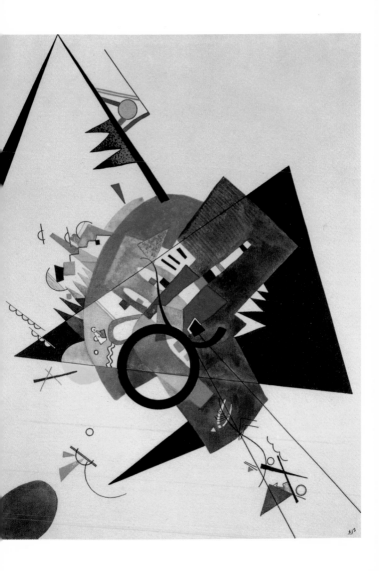

Wassily Kandinsky
Schwarzes Dreieck/Black Triangle, 1923
Privatsammlung/Private collection, Stuttgart, © VG Bild-Kunst, Bonn, 1993

Aus dem Prestel-Buch/From the Prestel book:
Kandinsky, Aquarelle und Zeichnungen/Kandinsky, Watercolors and Drawings
(German and English editions) Prestel, München · New York

Wassily Kandinsky
Strich zentraler/Central Line, 1924
Ingrid Hutton, New York, © VG Bild-Kunst, Bonn, 1993

Aus dem Prestel-Buch/From the Prestel book:
Kandinsky, Aquarelle und Zeichnungen/Kandinsky, Watercolors and Drawings
(German and English editions) Prestel, München · New York

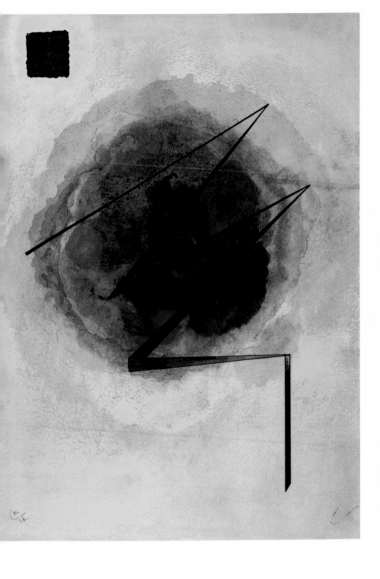

Wassily Kandinsky
Zickzack/Zigzag, 1926
Privatsammlung/Private collection, © VG Bild-Kunst, Bonn, 1993

Aus dem Prestel-Buch/From the Prestel book:
Kandinsky, Aquarelle und Zeichnungen/Kandinsky, Watercolors and Drawings
(German and English editions) Prestel, München · New York

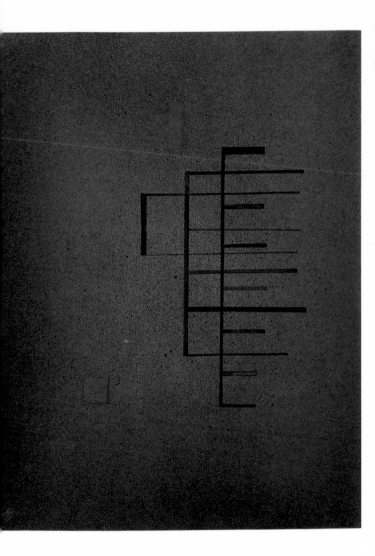

Wassily Kandinsky
Waagrecht Blau/Horizontal Blue, 1929
Hilla von Rebay Foundation, © VG Bild-Kunst, Bonn, 1993

Aus dem Prestel-Buch/From the Prestel book:
Kandinsky, Aquarelle und Zeichnungen/Kandinsky, Watercolors and Drawings
(German and English editions) Prestel, München · New York

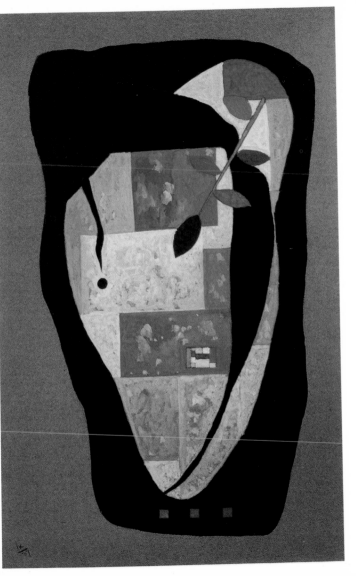

Wassily Kandinsky
Schwarz und kalt/Black and Cold, 1937
Privatsammlung/Private collection, © VG Bild-Kunst, Bonn, 1993

Aus dem Prestel-Buch/From the Prestel book:
Kandinsky, Aquarelle und Zeichnungen/Kandinsky, Watercolors and Drawings
(German and English editions) Prestel, München · New York

Wassily Kandinsky
Horizontales/Horizontal, 1939
Privatsammlung/Private collection, © VG Bild-Kunst, Bonn, 1993

Aus dem Prestel-Buch/From the Prestel book:
Kandinsky, Aquarelle und Zeichnungen/Kandinsky, Watercolors and Drawings
(German and English editions) Prestel, München · New York